Higgins PT Boat

Written by David Doyle

On Deck

658

658

658

Squadron Signal Publications

Cover Art by Don Greer

Line Illustrations by Melinda Turnage

(Front Cover) PT-285 of Squadron 23 speeds out on its shakedown cruise off the entrance to the Miami Yacht Harbor, Florida.

(Back Cover) Assigned to Squadron 17, PT-234 displays a two-color camouflage scheme as well as numerous modifications. In addition to the early-model radar mast, a 40mm Bofors gun has been mounted on the fantail. Two Mk. 13 torpedoes are in their racks and a single depth charge is to the rear of each torpedo.

About the On Deck Series®

The On Deck® series is about the details of specific military ships using color and black-and-white archival photographs and photographs of in-service, preserved, and restored equipment. *On Deck*® titles are picture books devoted to warships.

Hardcover ISBN 978-0-89747-655-3
Softcover ISBN 978-0-89747-654-6

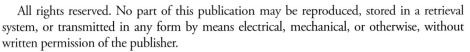

Proudly printed in the U.S.A.
Copyright 2012 Squadron/Signal Publications
1115 Crowley Drive, Carrollton, TX 75006-1312 U.S.A.
www.SquadronSignalPublications.com

Military/Combat Photographs and Snapshots

If you have any photos of aircraft, armor, soldiers, or ships of any nation, particularly wartime snapshots, please share them with us and help make Squadron/Signal's books all the more interesting and complete in the future. Any photograph sent to us will be copied and returned. Electronic images are preferred. The donor will be fully credited for any photos used. Please send them to the address above.

(Title Page) Only a handful of the 209 PT Boats built by Higgins Industries survive today. Of this select group, only PT-658, painstakingly restored by Save the PT Boat, Inc., is in operational condition. (Jim Alexander)

Acknowledgments

This book would not have been possible without the restoration and preservation efforts of PT Boats, Inc., Save the PT Boat, Inc, the Defenders of America Naval Museum, and the National Museum of the Pacific War. The considerable assistance of Tom Kailbourn, David E. Harper, Jim Alexander, the Military Vehicle Preservation Association, and the entire staff at Squadron/Signal Publications were instrumental in creating this volume. The meaning of the support, suggestions, and patience given by my wife Denise as we drove the 7,100-mile odyssey to take these photos cannot be put into words.

Introduction

Work in the United States began on Patrol Torpedo, or PT, boats in the 1930s. These boats were intended to be used as high-speed, nighttime raiders, able to quickly sneak, deliver a heavy punch to the enemy, and withdraw before the came under attack themselves. By the late 1930s a number of designs, by a number of firms, had been trialed by the US Navy. Two manufacturers stood out, the Electric Launch Corporation (ELCO) and Higgins Industries, of New Orleans, Louisiana. Owned by Andrew Jackson Higgins, a man who felt the talent of his firm, both in engineering and production, was second to none, Higgins Industries eschewed the designs of others, and created their own.

The 78-foot Higgins boats, while lacking the graceful lines of the ELCO, were notably rugged, and while Higgins crews had a bit wetter ride than their counterparts riding on Bayonne-built boats, they had the tactical advantage of a more maneuverable boat. Ultimately, only 209 78-foot PTs were built by Higgins, vs. 326 80-foot ELCO boats. Despite this, more Higgins-built boats survive today, although this numbers fewer than a half dozen. Although all the production Higgins boats can be considered the PT-71 class, there were notable variations through the production run. This book will examine the early Higgins PT boat, as exemplified by PT-309 at the National Museum of the Pacific War, Fredericksburg, Texas, as well as the late-style Higgins boat, primarily through photos of PT-658 in Portland, Oregon, augmented by photos of PT Boats, Inc.'s PT-796, displayed at Battleship Cove in Fall River, Massachusetts.

PT-84 was photographed on 8 December 1942, the day after she was placed into U.S. Navy service. Assigned to Squadron 13, she saw action in the Aleutians and the Southwest Pacific. She presents a good idea of an early-production Higgins 78-foot PT boat as originally configured, with an uncluttered foredeck, four torpedo tubes, and no radar mast. (PT Boats, Inc.)

Placed into service on 20 October 1943, PT-297 was a 78-foot Higgins-built PT boat that served with Squadron 16 in the Southwest Pacific in 1944 and 1945. It had a two-color camouflage scheme and carried four torpedo tubes with compressed air flasks on top. Oerlikon 20mm cannons were on the foredeck and fantail. The machine gun turrets are abreast of the bridge, their location until they were moved aft with the PT-450–485 class. (PT Boats, Inc.)

Four early-production Higgins 78-foot PT boats are moored together and their crews are conferring on the foredeck of the farthest boat. The boats have been fitted with folding windshields as well as covers over the chart-house windows to eliminate telltale glare. The closest boat has a cover installed over the bridge. The last boat in line has an early-model radar mast. (Stan Piet)

PT-81, which would serve with Squadron 13, was photographed on the occasion of her commissioning in December 1942. The circular device on the turret was the insignia of the mosquito boats, a cartoon of a mosquito riding on a torpedo that is about to splash into the water. Watertight covers are fitted over the turrets (with fully elevated guns) and the fronts of the torpedo tubes. (PT Boats, Inc.)

4

PT-212 maneuvers into a floating dry dock at La Maddalena, Sardinia, in 1944. This boat saw combat in the Mediterranean with Squadron 15 before being transferred to the British under Land-Lease in mid-October 1944. Visible are canvas spray shields in front of the turrets, a weatherproof cover over the fully elevated port .50-caliber machine guns, and two launching racks for Mk. 13 torpedoes. (PT Boats, Inc.)

Attached to Squadron 20, PT-252 served in the South Pacific and Southwest Pacific areas. Her 37mm cannon on the foredeck was equipped with an armored shield. In addition to her normal complement of weapons, twin 50-caliber machine guns and a 60mm mortar were mounted on the foredeck, and two .30-caliber machine guns on pedestal mounts were aft of the turret. (PT Boats, Inc.)

PT-252's additional weapons turned her into a virtual gunboat. The 37mm cannon, topped with an empty magazine, is at the far left. The 60mm mortar is next to the cannon. Large ammunition boxes flank the machine guns. The muzzles of the .50s on the bow and in the turret sport flash suppressors. Standing behind the Mk. 13 torpedo is a gunner manning a pedestal-mounted .30-caliber machine gun. (PT Boats, Inc.)

A third view of PT-252 was taken from amidships toward the bridge. The engine room cover has been opened, revealing its framing. A recognition star is painted on the deck and engine room cover; parts of the star are visible. Aft of the bridge are two oil drums and a deck vent that has been removed from its mount. To the right is a pedestal-mounted .30-caliber machine gun. (PT Boats, Inc.)

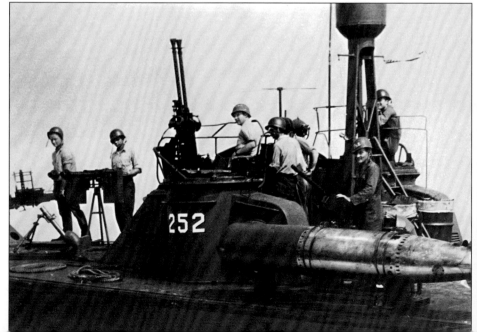

Higgins boats of the PT-625–660 class came from the factory with a Mk. 50 5-inch rocket launcher on each side of the main deck forward of the chart house. Each launcher held eight rockets and pivoted out away from the hull for firing. The launcher was manually elevated using the crank near the top and was fired electrically from the bridge. The direction of the boat controlled traverse. (PT Boats, Inc.)

PT-459 had suffered damage to its bow when it was photographed undergoing repairs in a floating dry dock at Cherbourg, France, in the last year of World War II. This boat was placed into service with Motor Torpedo Boat Squadron (or Ron) 30 on 23 March 1944, and saw combat in the English Channel between June 1944 and June 1945. (PT Boats, Inc.)

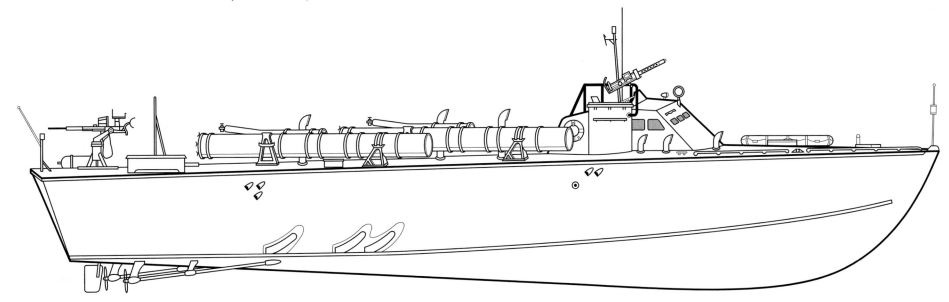

This Higgins 78-foot PT boat in Salerno Bay was painted in a "zebra" camouflage scheme. Applied experimentally to a small number of Higgins and Elco PT boats, the black and white stripes were intended to confuse enemy gunners as to the bearing, shape, and type of the boat. On the port side of the foredeck is a "Mousetrap" launcher that could fire four 4.5-inch rockets. (PT Boats, Inc.)

PT-452 was a member of the PT-450–485 class of Higgins boats. It was with this class that the machine gun turrets were relocated aft of the bridge. This boat had two launching racks for Mk. 13 torpedoes on both sides, six windows in the front of the chart house and two on each side of it, and two 20mm Oerlikon cannons aft of the engine room cover. (PT Boats, Inc.)

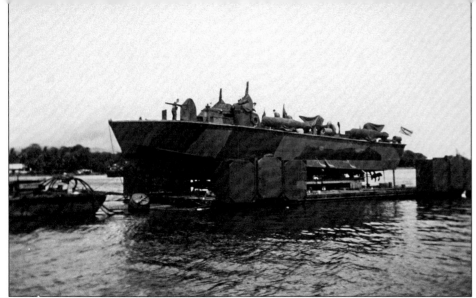

PT-227 was photographed in dry dock at the Pearl City Yacht Club on Oahu. She is painted in a Measure 31 camouflage scheme, and all guns and torpedoes are covered. This boat was assigned to Squadron 17 and arrived in the Philippines in late 1944, where she served with distinction. PT-227 was honored in a Navy Unit Commendation for actions at Mindoro. (PT Boats, Inc.)

A photograph of the top of the chart house of what appears to be a PT-450–485 class boat indicates the locations of: the siren with a weather cover (1), IFF (identification, friend or foe) antenna (2), torpedo-director stand (3), cowling over the throttles and telegraph (also called annunciator) (4), and signaling searchlight fitted with a weather cover (5). (PT Boats, Inc.)

This photo was taken to document wind-deflector gear fitted to the Higgins PT boat in the foreground, evidently of the PT-450–485 class. A wind deflector has been fastened to the upper front edges of the windscreen, and a hinged Plexiglas windshield is on top of the windscreen. Canvas panels have also been lashed to the tops of the bridge bulwarks. The farthest boat's three-digit number begins with 45. (PT Boats, Inc.)

Features in the bridge of a Higgins boat, probably of the PT-450–485 class, include the flux-gate compass (1), Pioneer compass (2), throttle and telegraph assembly (3), instrument panel (4), speaking tube (5), torpedo-director stand (6), searchlight (7), and TCS radio remote-control door (8). To the port side of the searchlight is the antenna and insulated support. (PT Boats, Inc.)

9

The bridge of a PT-625–660 class boat is displayed. Each grip on the helm of early Higgins PT boats had a deep, decorative groove near the base that tended to snap off under hard use. In June 1944 these handles were simplified without the grooves, as seen here. The gauge forward of the helm was the rudder angle indicator. The control panel next to the helm was of a different design than the one on early Higgins boats. (PT Boats, Inc.)

A Higgins Industries photo taken in early 1945 illustrates the controls on the port side of the bridge of a PT-625–660 class boat. Instrument lights with coiled power cords are clipped next to the flux-gate compass and the instrument panel. The square plate to the far right is the mount for the torpedo director in its folded-down position. Also visible are two hand rails. (PT Boats, Inc.)

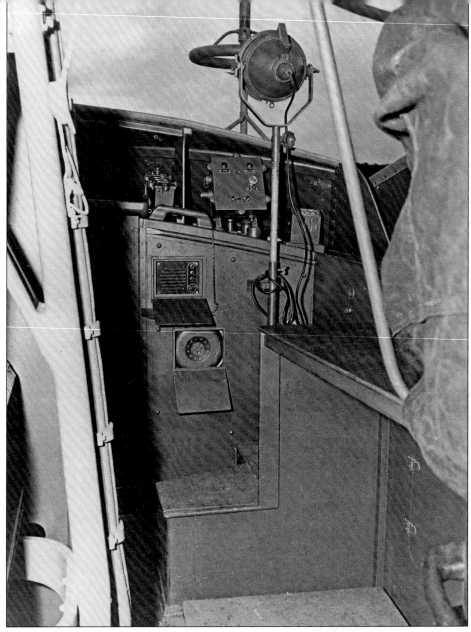

This factory photo of the starboard side of the bridge of a PT-625–660 class boat shows the TCS radio remote control and speaker unit with its door open, as well as several late-production additions. The large box to the upper right of the remote control is the firing panel for the Mk. 50 5-inch rocket launchers. To the left of that panel is the firing panel for the torpedo-launching racks. To the left of the photo is the starboard side of the radar antenna mast. To the right is part of the starboard turret and its weather cover; note the hand rail on the side of the turret. On top of the chart house forward of the searchlight is the IFF antenna. (PT Boats, Inc.)

As seen on a PT-625–660 class boat, the signaling searchlight was on an adjustable stanchion and could be adjusted so the light was below the windscreen or extended above it. Below the windscreen to the front of the searchlight are the torpedo rack launcher panel and rocket-launching control panel. On this class of boats the radio antenna was outside of the bridge.

Taken at the boatyard at Higgins Industries in New Orleans in March 1945, this view of PT-631 is facing aft from the front of the starboard Mk. 50 5-inch rocket launchers, in their stowed position. On the chart house roof (right) are a hand rail, ventilator with a weather cover, and the IFF antenna. In the left background are two unfinished PT boat hulls. (PT Boats, Inc.)

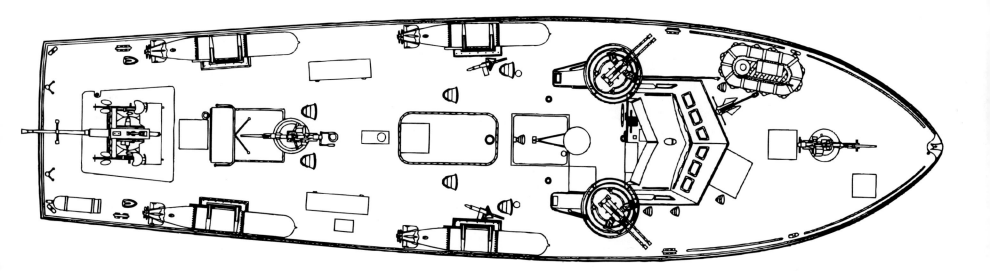

Numbered elements in this photo of a Higgins PT boat with a radar mast in the foreground include the hatch to the wardroom (1), conning stand (2), conning seat (3), small-arms locker (4), helmsman's locker (5), locker for proposed MN phone (6), searchlight (7), signal gear locker under conning stand (8), and door for TCS radio speaker and remote control (9). (PT Boats, Inc.)

Whereas the PT-625–660 class had ventilation louvers on the insides of the bulwarks aft of the turrets, earlier classes of Higgins 78-foot boats, such as this example apparently from the PT-450–485 class, had rectangular louvers on the aft faces of the bulwarks. Their heights are not equal. In the foreground is the radome of an early-model radar mast in the lowered position. (PT Boats, Inc.)

At the top of the SO-3 radar mast of a PT-625–660 class boat is the CRP-66AGF antenna assembly, while near the bottom of the mast is the CPR-43ACD transmitter-receiver. In the foreground is the cradle, in which the mast rested when lowered. Aft of the bridge is a bulkhead of ¼-inch armor, part of the bridge armor suite introduced on this class of boats. (PT Boats, Inc.)

Numbered features in this view toward the bridge of a late Higgins PT boat are: locker for electrical shore lead (1), locker for two submachine guns and four .30-caliber carbines (2), helmsman's locker (3), locker for proposed MN phone (4), flux-gate compass (5), Pioneer compass (6), throttles (7), and unassigned stowage space (8). Mounted near the base of the folded-down mast is the radar transmitter-receiver unit. (PT Boats, Inc.)

Looking aft and starboard from the bridge of a late Higgins PT boat are: stowage locker for fenders, lead lines, etc. (1), sound-powered telephone locker (2), conning seat (3), searchlight (4), wardroom hatch (5), locker for signal gear (6), and removable step in the turret to provide clearance for a funnel for the fuel filler (7). In earlier Higgins boats the turret was abreast of the bridge. (PT Boats, Inc.)

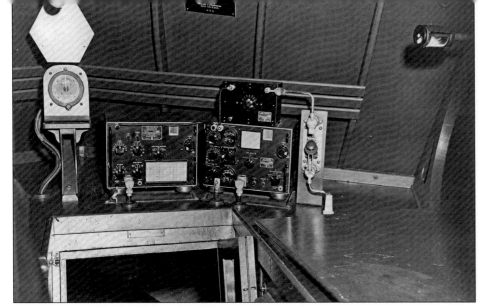

Inside the chart house of PT-631 facing forward, the master indicator for the gyrocompass is on its foundation shelf to the left. To the right of it are, left to right, the Type COL-46159 radio receiver and the Type COL-52245 radio transmitter, on top of which is the Type COL-47205 antenna loading coil. Above the radio are nameplates and data plates. The hatch to the crew quarters and galley is at the bottom left. (PT Boats, Inc.)

On the port side of the chart house of PT-631 are, left to right: the Type 55ADQ radar plan position indicator, above which is the Type 23AEE radar accessory control unit; the Type 23AEJ bearing control unit; the gyrocompass master indicator; and radio receiver. At the top center are a light and an electric fan—a necessity, as the vacuum tubes of the electronics equipment could get very warm. (PT Boats, Inc.)

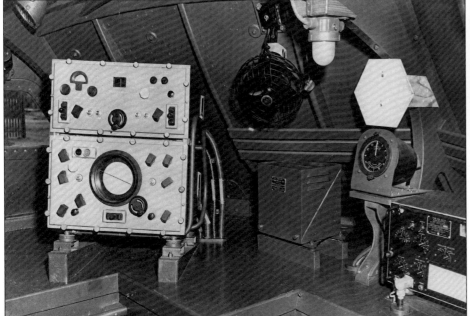

The wardroom was a combination officers' sleeping quarters, office, and mess hall. This compartment also held some of the electronics equipment. The box mounted to the aft bulkhead, and adjacent to the berth, is the CRP-20247 rectifier power unit (RPU) of the radar system. The larger box mounted on the rack below it is the CFN-10233 BN unit, part of the IFF (identification, friend or foe) system, which interfaced with the radar system. The small box on the bulkhead between the RPU and the BN unit is the voltage regulator, again part of the radar electronics. The ladder led to a hatch to the starboard rear of the bridge. To the right are the hatch to the officers' head, a chair, and the desk. (PT Boats, Inc.)

17

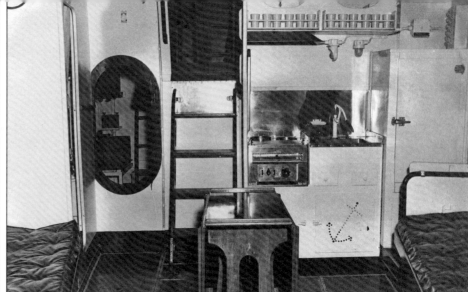

Viewing aft from the forward part of the crew quarters of a PT-625–660 class boat, the drop-leaf mess table is in the foreground. This table had raised edges, to keep dinnerware from sliding off. Transom berths with Pantasote upholstery are on each side. At the aft end of the compartment are, left to right, the crew's head, hatch to the wardroom, ladder to the chart house, and galley. (PT Boats, Inc.)

The 78-foot Higgins PT boats, including this example from the PT-625–660 class, had three propellers and two rudders. The three shiny square plates on the hull above the rudders are the zincs, while faintly visible above the propellers are the erosion plates. These features were designed to protect the rudders and propellers from destruction from galvanic action. (PT Boats, Inc.)

In this close-up view of the galley, the stove and sink with a faucet powered by a hand pump are mounted on a cabinet, with the refrigerator/freezer to the right. With these appliances, a good cook could whip up excellent meals when provisions were abundant. Ventilation holes in the form of decorative anchors were drilled in the cabinet doors, and the stove had an exhaust vent, the duct for which is visible inside the cupboard above the stove. At the top right is an electric fan, one of numerous ones inside the boat. Proper ventilation below decks was a constant concern in warm climates, since the action of a hot sun beating down on a hull all day long could make the interior insufferably hot and humid. (PT Boats, Inc.)

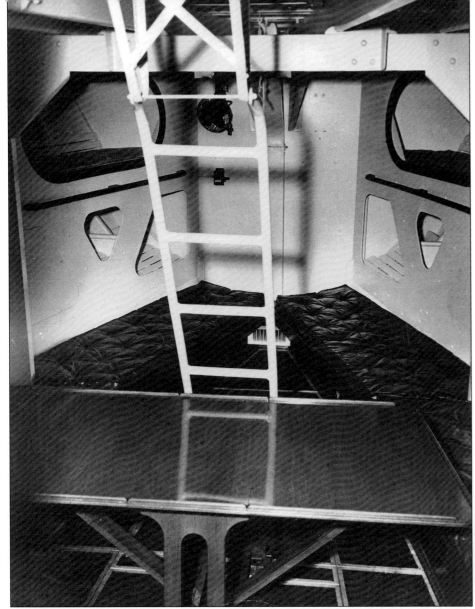

From the aft part of the crew compartment of a PT-625–660 class boat, the mess table is shown with the leaves raised. Above is an aluminum ladder suspended from brackets; it was raised and secured when not in use and provided access to the crew compartment hatch on the foredeck. Forward of the ladder are the aluminum beams and stanchions installed in this class of Higgins PT boats to reinforce the wooden frame of the foredeck to support the weight of the 37mm cannon. In the forward part of the compartment, berths are situated behind the longitudinal bulkheads. Below these berths, cutouts in the longitudinal bulkheads provided access to stowage spaces between these bulkheads and the hull. (PT Boats, Inc.)

The ammunition locker jutted into the forward part of the wardroom. It was used not only to store ammunition, but also spare gun barrels, spare parts, and other essentials. There were also ammunition stowage lockers on the main deck. Racks were built into the locker, and it was painted white. The locker door, to the left, was 47.5 inches high by 19.5 inches wide and was made of ⅞-inch mahogany plywood. Above is a hand rail made of mahogany. On the floor of the locker are several .50-caliber ammunition trays for the turrets; they were shaped to fit alongside the curved wall of a turret. To the right are small-arms racks. These racks could hold a combination of rifles, carbines, or submachine guns, all useful for close-in action or shore patrols. (PT Boats, Inc.)

As seen from the starboard side of the center engine (lower left), the forward bulkhead of the engine compartment is in the background, with the instrument panel flanked by the freshwater expansion tanks. Below the instrument panel are the fuel manifold and fuel pumps. Above the starboard engine (upper right) is a ventilation duct with a screen over the opening. (PT Boats, Inc.)

The aft part of the engine room of a PT-625–660 class boat is pictured, with the front end of the center engine behind the ladder leading to the main deck and all three transmission gearshift levers in the foreground. The generator and distribution switchboard is to the far left, while a battery box is at both aft corners of the compartment. (PT Boats, Inc.)

The starboard wing Packard 4M-2500 engine of a Higgins 78-foot PT boat is viewed from the aft end. At the upper forward end of the engine are the air cleaner and coolant lines. To the right are the two carbon dioxide bottles of the fixed fire extinguisher system as well as the starboard longitudinal bulkhead with its triangular cutouts. Fastened to the bulkhead at the upper left is the fuel manifold. (PT Boats, Inc.)

On both sides of the aft part of the engine room of the PT-625–660 class Higgins boat was a 5.5-kilowatt auxiliary gasoline engine/generator with a control panel above it on the longitudinal bulkhead; these ones are on the port side. The auxiliary generators were used to provide electricity to the boat when the main engines were not running, and they also powered the appliances in the galley. At times, to provide necessary electrical power to the communications equipment, it was necessary to shut down power to the galley. Above the auxiliary engine/generator control box is a telephone junction box and portable fire extinguisher. To the left are the port battery box, a workbench with a vise, and, at the top left, a rag locker. (PT Boats, Inc.)

Part of the PT-295–313 class of Higgins 78-foot boats, PT-309 was placed into service on 26 January 1944. Nicknamed *Oh Frankie,* PT-309 of Squadron 22 served in the Mediterranean in World War II, operating under British coastal forces off the South of France and northwest Italy and offering support to the invasion of Elba in June 1944. The boat has an early-model radar mast with a two-tone radome. On the foredeck are a 20mm cannon, a life raft, and rope fender. (PT Boats, Inc.)

PT-309 is currently on indoor display at the Nimitz Museum of the Pacific War, Fredericksburg, Texas. PT-309 was one of a handful of PT boats to survive World War II. The nickname *Oh Frankie* came from a chance meeting of her skipper with Frank Sinatra at a nightclub in New York City. The boat saw heavy combat in the Mediterranean and was credited with sinking five enemy ships.

To the port side of the centerline of the foredeck of PT-309 is a Mk. 4 20mm Oerlikon cannon. Aft of the mannequin is the chart house. When the lights in the chart house were lit at night, windows without blackout covers made the boat an easy target.

The base of the 20mm cannon mount, in this case a tripod-type Mk. 10 mount, was attached to a rectangular, wooden foundation secured to the deck. Beyond the foundation is the hatch to the crew's quarters and a life raft.

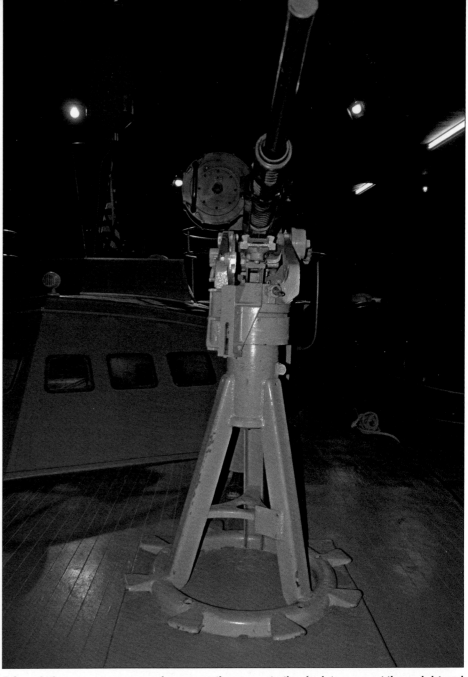

A foundation was necessary when mounting a gun to the deck to prevent the weight and stresses of the piece during firing from damaging the deck planking. The round front face of the 60-round magazine with its grab handle is in view. A wound clock spring inside the 20mm magazine maintained constant feed pressure on the ammunition as it made its way through spiral tracks inside the magazine.

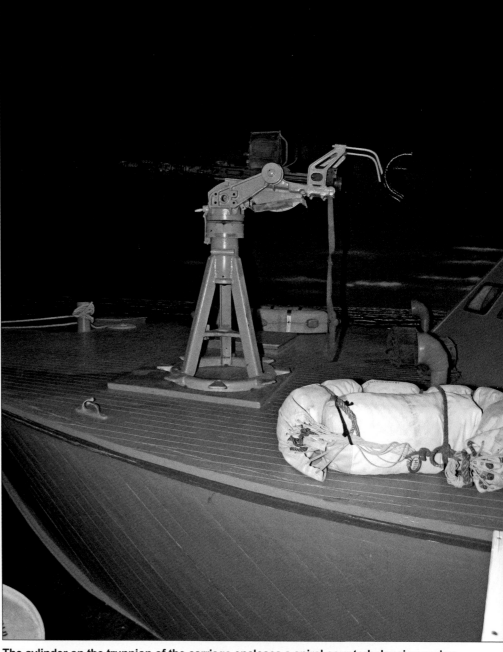

The receiver of the 20mm cannon fits onto a cradle, which, in turn, is suspended in the trunnions of the carriage on top of the stand, in this case a tripod. The cradle, carriage, and stand comprise the mount. Several different types of 20mm gun mounts were used on Higgins PT boats during World War II. The small cylinder on front of the carriage is the carriage lock lever, which kept the gun from traversing when the lever was engaged.

The cylinder on the trunnion of the carriage encloses a spiral counterbalancing spring, which exerted torsion on the gun to overcome the imbalance in the weight of the mounted gun. The spring mechanism made it easier for the gunner to elevate the gun. Note the deck planking, installed fore-to-aft, and the diagonal planking on the side of the hull. Substantial parts of the planking have been replaced. (David E. Harper)

The belt dangling below the rear of the cradle was for strapping the gunner secure to the shoulder rests. Normally, a spent-cartridge collector bag would have been attached below the cradle. (David E. Harper)

Two 20mm magazines are resting on the deck next to the port side of the chart house. A makeshift Plexiglas panel has been screwed over the forward side window. Note the trim pieces on the corner and bottom of the chart house.

PT-309's forward 20mm cannon is fitted with shoulder rests. A photograph of this boat in the Mediterranean in World War II indicates that, rather than shoulder rests, this gun had a tall, curved handlebar rising above the aft end of the gun.

During its war service, PT-309 had a locker for 20mm ammunition to the front starboard side of the chart house, and probably one on the port side; these are presently missing. Note the deck vent in the corner between the chart house and the turret.

As viewed from the bridge with the horn in the foreground, the hatch to the crew's quarters is at the center, and the open hatch to the forepeak, a compartment where anchor cables and other items were stowed, is to the front of the life raft.

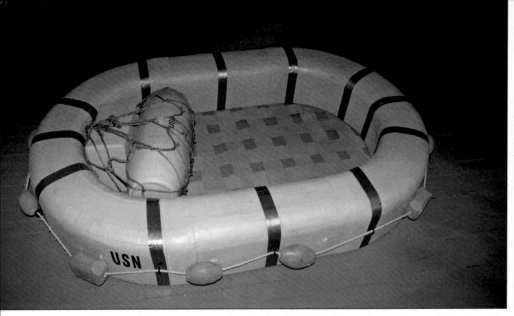

A replica life raft is stowed on the foredeck of PT-309. A wooden water cask is stored in the raft. PT-boat life rafts were more of a flotation device to give crewmen something to hold onto and to stow survival gear in, than to sit in.

With the addition of a 20mm cannon to the foredecks of Higgins PT boats beginning in 1943, the boats could direct an impressive amount of firepower toward the front. With the later additions of rocket launchers and 37mm guns, this firepower would increase exponentially.

In a view inside the forepeak, the slotted floor panels allowed water that entered the compartment to flow to the bilge. The diagonal arrangement of the inner layer of hull planking and the vertical row of rivets that helped hold the inner and outer layers of planking together are visible.

The port side of PT-309 is shown in perspective, with the Mk. 13 torpedo visible amidships. The tops of the reproduction turrets and the depression rails now installed vary slightly from their World War II appearances.

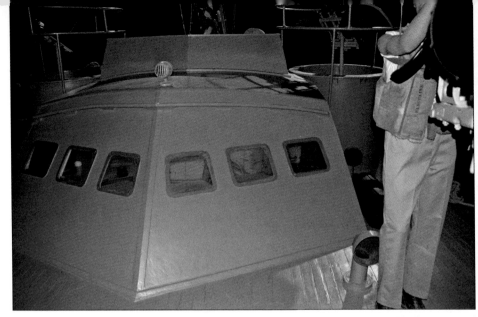

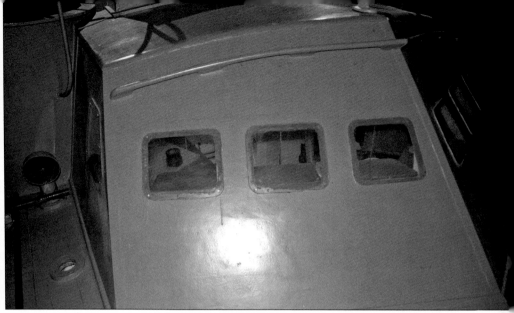

The chart house of the Higgins 78-foot PT boats was easily distinguishable from that of the Elco 80-foot PT boats by the two forward bulwarks that came to a point at the center, as opposed to the single forward bulwark of the Elco chart house. Aft of the roof of the chart house is the windscreen of the bridge.

A deck vent is on each side just forward of the chart house. The thumbscrews were loosened to rotate the vent or remove it. During the war, the inside of the vent would not have been painted red: building instructions for PT boats expressly prohibited the use of red paint topsides.

PT-309's chart house windows originally comprised Plexiglas panels in metal frames. Sometime during the war, the Plexiglas panels were painted over to eliminate telltale glare. Across the top of the front of the chart house are hand rails; they were made from solid mahogany.

The navigation horn was fastened to the forward center part of the roof of the chart house. It was a watertight, 24-volt unit, operated by a push-button on the electrical switch panel on the bridge. In addition to its signaling use to other craft, the horn could serve as a cease-fire signal to the gunners.

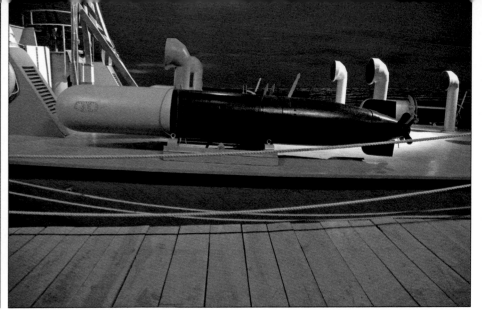

The port side of the chart house, bridge, and port turret are displayed. The turrets are located to the sides of the bridge; in late-production Higgins PT boats, the turrets would be moved to aft of the bridge. Twin .50-caliber machine guns with dual hand grips on each receiver are on inaccurate, makeshift mounts with ammunition boxes to the sides.

A Mk. 13 torpedo is resting in a launching rack amidships. The metal rack is fastened to a wooden foundation pad on the deck. To the left, ventilating louvers are visible at the aft ends of the bulwarks. Between the bulwarks are the radar mast and its support. Tall deck ventilators are also in view.

In the chart house, a mannequin gazes toward the windows, which are fitted with hinged blackout blinds and hold-open chains. To the left is the radar console, comprising the Type 23AEE radar accessory control unit mounted atop the Type 55ADQ radar plan position indicator.

Details of the framing, corner brace, and blackout blinds on the starboard side of the chart house interior are visible. As originally configured, a radio transmitter and chart board would have been on this part of the desk. A hand lantern and megaphone are on the desk.

A view from the aft port side of PT-309 reveals, left to right, a Mk. 13 torpedo, the aft torpedo launching rack, and a depth charge in a roll-off rack. Forward of the 40mm gun is the hatch to the stowage compartment and lazarette. In the background is the bridge with a mannequin at the helm.

The port aft launching rack is shown in close-up. The lever in the foreground released the cables and retainers that held the torpedo secure. This was accomplished through the rods and linkages visible between the cradles of the rack. Toward the upper right is the engine room cover.

A release rack for a depth charge is on each side of PT-309 toward the stern. To the right of it is a rack for 40mm ammunition containers, one of the lids for which is lying next to the rack on the deck. At the lower right is the wooden foundation for the 40mm Bofors gun.

A Mk. 13 torpedo is shown in a launching rack on the starboard side of PT-309. The warhead is to the left. Steel cables would have been used to secure the torpedo in the rack. When photographed in port in the Mediterranean in the latter part of World War II, this boat had four torpedo racks.

The smoke generator rests in its wooden cradle in the aft part of PT-309. This device was an important part of the PT boat's defenses. A crewman operated it by opening a valve three full turns. When not in use, it was necessary to seal the nozzle with a rubber cover to prevent clogging.

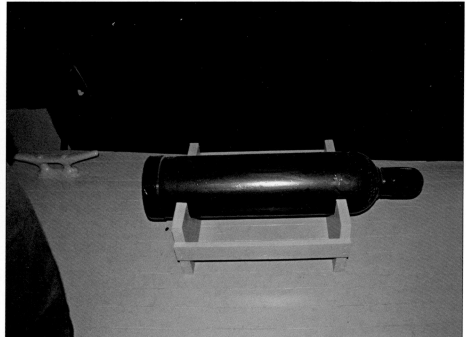

Whereas late-production Higgins PT boats with 40mm guns had wooden lockers on deck for stowing ammunition, PTs 308–313 and 456–461 had racks made of galvanized angle irons, flat bars, and pipes. The racks held the watertight metal 40-mm ammunition shipping containers. Each of these ammunition boxes was filled with 16 rounds in four four-round clips, ready to use.

A number of 40mm ammunition containers are sitting in the racks. In the original 40mm ammunition racks, steel hooks secured the handles on the sides of the ammunition containers to the racks; the lower end of each hook was threaded, and a wing nut held the hook snugly to the rack.

The 40mm ammunition container racks on PT-309 are replicas made of wood. Here, two four-round clips of 40mm ammunition are propped up on top of an open ammunition container sitting inside one of the racks. The green/white/red markings on the rounds in the foreground are indicative of High-Explosive Incendiary Tracer, Self-Destruct rounds, while the green/white/green markings on those in the background indicate High-Explosive Tracer, Self-Destruct rounds.

Specifications

Length	78 feet 9 inches
Beam	20 feet 1 inch
Displacement	48 tons
Draft	5 feet 3 inches
Powerplant	Three Packard 4M-2500 V-12 liquid-cooled engines, 1,200-1,500 h.p., each.
Armament	Two 22.4-inch diameter Mk13 torpedoes on roll-off racks; two twin .50-cal. machine guns; one 40mm gun; one 37mm gun; one 20mm gun; smoke generator; two Mark 50 5-inch rocket launchers.
Speed	39 knots
Range	550 miles
Crew	17

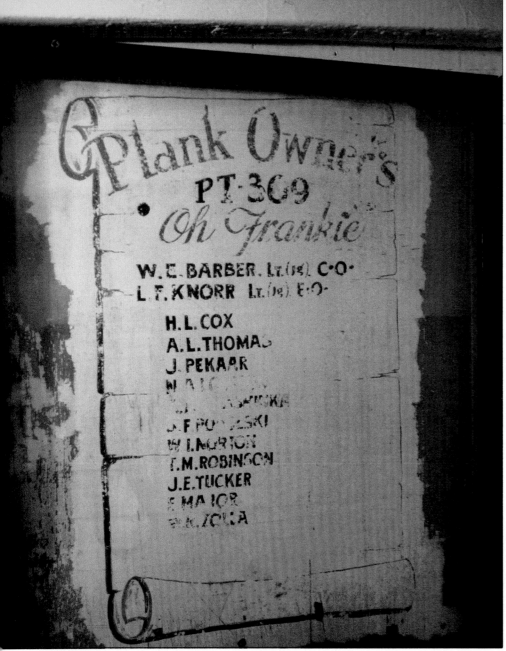

Discovered during the restoration of PT-309, this original graphic commemorates the boat's "plank owners," who comprised the original crew of the boat at the time of its commissioning. Topping the list is Lt. (j.g.) Wayne E. Barber, the commanding officer, followed by his executive officer, Lt. (j.g.) Lawrence F. Knorr. This WWII veteran PT-boat fired over 100 torpedoes during wartime and was credited with sinking five enemy ships.

One of the deck vents, also called a cowl vent, in the amidships area is shown in close-up. The shaft of the vent is mounted on a round metal flange attached to the deck, and each vent could be rotated on that flange to position the intake to draw in the most (or least, if desired) amount of air. The intake scoop at the top is multi-faceted, being fabricated from interlocking sections. In the background are the 40mm Bofors gun and one of the 40mm ammunition racks.

The exhaust mufflers on Higgins 78-foot PT boats were mounted just below the waterline on the sides of the hull. These were brass castings, three on each side, and each included a bronze butterfly valve inside. Each muffler was fastened to the hull with 35 brass machine screws and nuts.

The three starboard mufflers are in this view, facing aft. The two mufflers to the right were for the starboard engine, while the single muffler to the left was for the starboard exhaust line of the center engine. The port exhaust line of the center engine was routed to the aft port muffler.

A muffler is shown in close-up. The holes toward the upper part of the muffler were designed to prevent backfire suction. The diagonal arrangement of the outer layer of upper hull planking is evident. This outer layer was mahogany boards, ½-inch thick. To the bottom is the display cradle for the boat.

The spray rail, which followed the chine (the line along which the upper hull and lower hull meet), helped reduce the amount of spray churned up when the boat was proceeding at high speed. On the PT-295–313 and PT-450–485 classes, the spray rail comprised an oak outer rail and spruce inner rail.

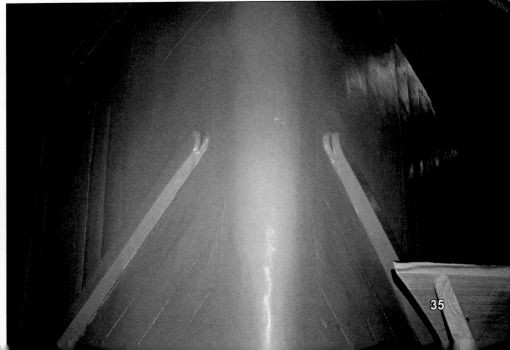

Manufactured at Higgins Industries' New Orleans plant and part of the PT-625–660 class, PT-658 was completed on 20 July 1945, a month before the end of World War II. The U.S. Navy reclassified her as a small boat in 1946 and as floating equipment in 1948, and ultimately sold the boat as surplus. Save the PT Boat, Inc., of Portland, Oregon, obtained custody of the boat in 1994 and continues to restore and display her. (Jim Alexander)

On the foredeck are the forepeak hatch (aft of the anchor) and crew quarters hatch (forward of the chart house). A life raft, an M4 20mm cannon, and a replica of an Oldsmobile 37mm cannon are also on the foredeck. Next to the port toe rail is a boat hook.

Mooring lines are lashed around the Samson post (also called the mooring bit) on the foredeck and pass through the fairlead, part of the bow cap assembly. A socket on top of the bow cap holds a simple wooden jack staff. This replaced the jack staff with a built-in bow navigation light used on earlier classes of Higgins PT boats.

The bow cap, incorporating the fairlead and socket for the jack staff of PT-658, is viewed from aft. Danforth anchors were usually used on PT boats in World War II. The anchor chain passes through the fairlead and disappears down the forepeak hatch.

PT-796's bow cap is viewed from aft. This is a correct type of bow cap for a late-production Higgins PT boat. The main casting was of molybdenum carbon steel. Note the deck planking.

The Samson post on Higgins PT boats was a wooden shaft, the lower part of which was anchored below deck. It was capped by a brass or bronze casting and had a metal crosspiece.

On the PT-625–660 class as issued, the 37mm gun was on a more substantial mount, which in turn was positioned on a built-up foundation on the deck, and the gun had a slightly different-shaped 30-round magazine.

The jack, comprising the blue field and stars of the national flag, hangs from the wooden jack staff at the bow of PT-658. Aft of it are the 37mm (left) and 20mm cannons, topped with their respective magazines. At the far left is the radar mast, with boat's bell visible.

The open hatch to the crew quarters is viewed from on top of the chart house. A small cable attached to the hatch holds it in an upright position. At the bottom of the photo are the hand rails on top of the front of the chart house.

In this overall view of the starboard side of the 37mm cannon on PT-658, it is noticeable that the deck is clad in plywood. Installed during restoration, this replaced the original deck of ⅜-inch mahogany planking covered by an intermediate layer of canvas duck coated with marine glue, and an outer layer of ½-inch by 2¾-inch mahogany planking.

The 20mm Oerlikon gun is on a makeshift tripod mount. The curved grips enabled the gunner to elevate the gun at a high angle without having to crouch. While some PT boats had a 20mm gun in this location, the boats of the PT-625–660 class had a Mk. 50 5-inch rocket launcher in this area on either side of the chart house.

The life raft was constructed of balsa wood wrapped with waterproofed muslin, with rope netting. These two-man life rafts were essentially intended to hold some survival supplies and give crewmen something to hold onto in the event they had to abandon ship. Late-war PT boats also carried two inflatable rafts.

Originally, the Higgins 78-foot PT boats had only one 20mm cannon, mounted on the fantail. As the war progressed and fewer Axis surface ships presented targets for the torpedoes, PT boats were increasingly turned into gunboats with the addition of 20mm and larger-caliber guns.

Fitted over the barrel to the front of the magazine is the barrel spring case; visible through its slots is the front barrel spring. Protruding from the top of the receiver to the rear of the magazine is the magazine catch lever, which actuated the locking of the magazine to the cannon.

PT-796 is fitted with a Mk. 4 20mm Oerlikon cannon on a Mk. 10 mount forward of the port side of the chart house. The Mk. 10 was a fixed-height mount, so, unlike some other 20mm mounts, the cradle and carriage could not be raised for ease of the gunner's elevating the cannon to a high angle. Adjustable shoulder rests are on the cradle to the rear of the cannon's receiver.

The Mk. 10 mount allowed the 20mm gun to elevate +90° and depress -15°. The eight tabs protruding from the rim of the base were foot rests; the gunner could plant his feet on or next to them to stabilize his stance when crouching to elevate the cannon.

The arrangement of the foredeck, chart house, bridge, and turrets of PT-658 is viewed from off the bow. The nearly horizontal hull planking was a feature of some late Higgins PT boats, as opposed to the diagonal layout on earlier classes of Higgins boats.

To the front of the chart house of PT-658 is a replica of an ammunition stowage box. PT-625–660 class Higgins boats sometimes had two such boxes to the front of the chart house – or no boxes at all.

With the PT-625–660 class, the windows were discontinued from the front of the chart-house. Specifications for the chart house called for ⅜-inch mahogany plywood on the top and ½-inch mahogany plywood on the front, sides, and back. (Jim Alexander)

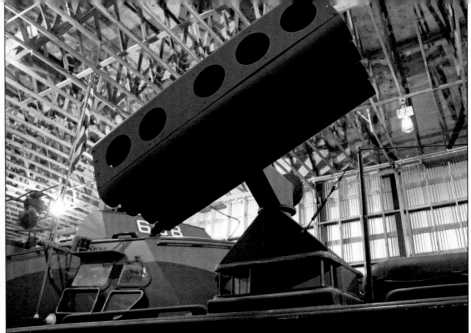

With no original Mk 50 rocket launchers available, the volunteers of Save the PT Boat fabricated detailed, full-size replicas in 2011. Now installed on PT-658, the depiction of the heavy armament carried by late-war PT boats is complete. (Jim Alexander).

On each side of the top of the chart house of PT-625-660 class boats, there was a cast-aluminum cowl vent with an oblong opening. The pattern number T-145C is cast on the flange of the vent. The pattern number of the vent itself is T-145.

Viewed from the port side of the chart house, the locations of the cowl vents are apparent, as is the pronounced grain of the well-weathered plywood. Photos of several wartime boats in the PT-625–660 class show a single horn on the port side of the top of the chart house.

The bottom and sides of the hull of the Higgins PT boat were sheathed with an inner layer of ⅜-inch by 5½-inch mahogany planking, covered with a layer of canvas duck (#10 on the sides and #12 on the bottom) impregnated with marine glue, and topped with ½-inch planking, 6⅛ inches to 13 inches wide. (Jim Alexander)

Looking across the top of the chart house from the starboard side, the plywood windscreen of bridge is to the left. This windscreen is a late version; earlier classes of Higgins PT boats lacked a top piece on the windscreen, and the front wings of the windscreen rose to a point at the center of the chart house.

The windows of the chart house have hinged covers with dogs (clamps) at the tops of the windows to secure them shut. On the platform over the windows is the starboard running light. The Monel antenna base of the TCS radio system is on the deck aft of the windows. Note the oblong vent and the torpedo to far left.

The starboard chart house windows, their covers, and the TCS antenna base are seen in close-up. The covers were intended to mask the glare of the glass of the windows and to blackout the interior of the chart house at night, since glare and interior lights could give away the presence of the boat to enemy gunners.

The searchlight was a combination spotlight and signal light. Toward the upper right are the masthead and anchor light and boat's bell, both of which are mounted on the early-type radar mast fitted to PT-658 during its restoration.

On Higgins PT-625–660 class boats, the searchlight was mounted in the bridge area on a stanchion at the starboard rear of the chart house. To the left is the depression rail of the starboard twin .50-caliber machine gun turret.

On PT-625–660 class boats, the searchlight and stanchion were secured to the chart house with a bracket toward the top of the chart house (not visible in this photo) and a flange on the floor of the bridge. By loosening a thumbscrew on the bracket, the stanchion and light could be raised and lowered.

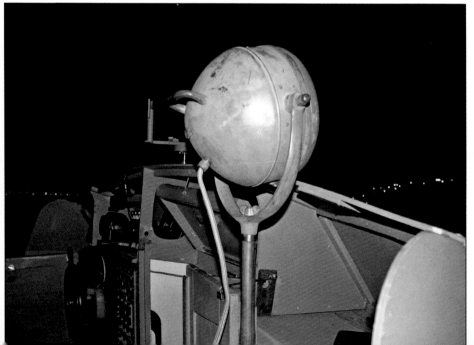

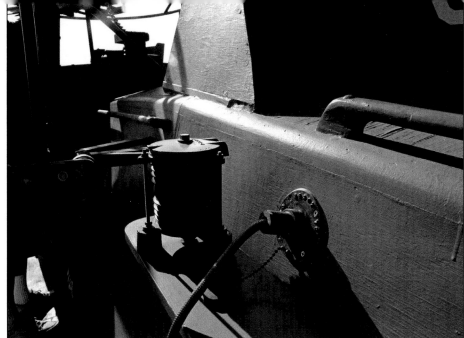

On the side of the chart house to the front of the green starboard navigation light is the receptacle for the power cord for that light. A red navigation light is in the corresponding location on the port side of the chart house.

Just aft of the starboard navigation light is the antenna for the TCS receiver-transmitter radio set. The antenna rests in a base on the deck and passes through the antenna support attached to the side of the chart house.

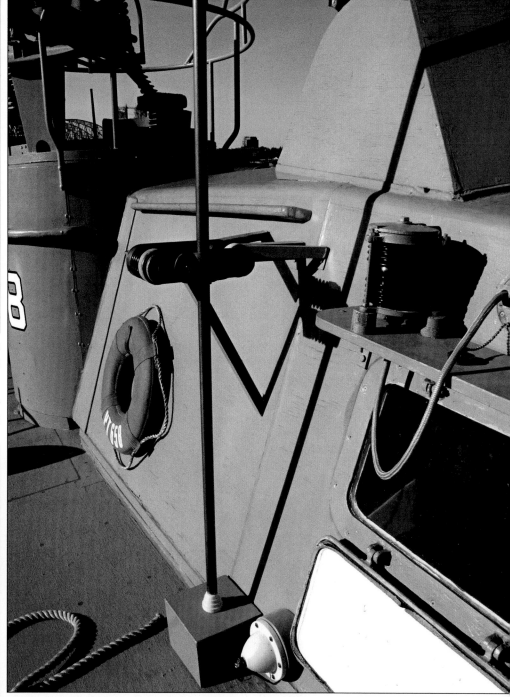

Viewing aft, the starboard navigation light is to the right, and the lower part of the TCS antenna, with its base and support assembly, are at the center. Aft of the antenna is a life preserver; these often had the number of the PT boat painted on them.

On the top housing of the starboard navigation light is the Bureau of Ships (BuShips) part number, 9-5-5498-L Alt-1. The port navigation light had the same BuShips number, as it was interchangeable with the starboard light.

The TCS Monel antenna (BuShips part number MM 435-X), support, and base are viewed from aft. At the bottom center is the antenna base, white base insulator, and another white insulator mounted on the side of the chart house through which the antenna cable passes.

The TCS antenna support includes two porcelain insulators sandwiched between a brass frame/clamp. The frame/insulators assembly in turn is attached to the starboard side of the chart house with a frame fabricated from aluminum angle irons.

The TCS antenna base, viewed from aft, was fabricated from welded aluminum plates. In actual practice in World War II, it is likely that the interiors of the window covers of the chart house would have been painted the same color as the exterior of the boat, rather than the more conspicuous white.

With the PT-450–485 class of Higgins boats, the two .50-caliber machine gun turrets, formerly situated to the sides of the bridge, were moved aft several feet, and this feature continued with the PT-625–660 class. The starboard turret on PT-658 is equipped with a full gun mount, including belted ammunition.

The exterior of the right side of the bridge is viewed from the starboard side of PT-658. Toward the top right are the side of the windscreen and top of the searchlight. Hand rails are provided on the side of the bridge and on the plywood turret. To the lower left is a ventilator.

The ventilator near the base of the starboard turret provided fresh air to the below decks, and could be rotated to draw in more, or less, air. The sides of the turrets were formed from curved pieces of plywood.

Viewed from the aft starboard side, the radar mast on PT-658 represents an early type discontinued by the time the PT-625–660 class was begun. That class, including PT-658, originally would have been fitted with a much different, late-war style of radar mast.

A gunner mans the starboard twin Browning M2 .50-caliber machine guns of an early-model Higgins 78-foot PT boat stationed in the Panama Canal Zone in January 1943. The guns are seated on the Mk. 9 cradle (which includes the curved hand grips), part of the Mk. 17 gun mount. The flex tube below the guns is the spent-cartridge chute.

This is a gunner's-eye view of the interior of a turret on PT-658. The ammunition boxes for .50-caliber ammunition are to the left and right, and the pedestal of the gun carriage is at the center. The metal parts of the turret below the Mk. 9 gun cradle are designated the Mk. 9 gun carriage; together, the cradle and carriage comprise the Mk. 17 gun mount.

The framework of the starboard side of the starboard Mk. 17 .50-caliber gun mount is displayed. The Mk 17 Scarff mounts, named for their inventor, F. W. Scarff, were furnished by the Government to Higgins for installation on the boats. To the front of the turret is the side of the chart house, with the open covers for the side windows visible.

As seen from the rear of the twin .50-caliber machine gun mount, the gunner's cradle-shaped back rest is in the foreground. The gunner manually traversed the gun mount by pushing the back from side to side with his upper body, and he could also swing the gun cradle from side to side.

Two lower guide assemblies are attached to the brace tubes of the .50-caliber machine gun mounts, to properly direct the linked ammunition from the ammunition boxes up to the upper guides and thence to the guns. The guide at the center is on the port side of the starboard turret, with the gunner's back rest to the right.

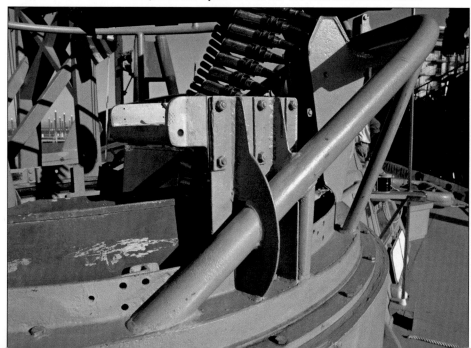

This overhead view shows the respective locations of the two twin-.50-caliber machine gun turrets on the PT-450–485 and later classes. On the Higgins 78-foot PT boat classes prior to the PT-450–485 class, the turrets were located abreast of the bridge, in the area where the life preserver is stowed.

PT-658 is furnished with four Mk. 13 torpedoes in roll-off racks, a misnomer, since the torpedoes slid, rather than rolled, off the racks. This configuration replaced the bulky torpedo tubes mounted on early Higgins 78-foot PT boats. At the center is the forward starboard torpedo, with the side of the turret to the right.

As viewed from the area to the rear of the bridge, the inner side of the starboard turret is at the center. Below the hand rail on the side of the turret is the hatch whereby the gunner entered the turret. Note the louvered vent on the superstructure to the right.

The torpedo roll-off racks (also called torpedo release gear; the starboard aft one is shown) were mounted on wooden foundations, also referred to as pads. The cables held the torpedoes in their racks until the moment of launching.

Once the cables were released and the torpedo motor was started, a torpedoman rolled the torpedo off the side by manually operating a lever which lowered the hinged retainers that held the torpedo in place in the rack; one support is visible to the right.

On World War II PT boats, Mk. 13 torpedoes lacked the shroud ring on the fins, as this feature was intended for aircraft-delivered torpedoes. Round access panels for various mechanisms are on the warhead and casing of the torpedo.

51

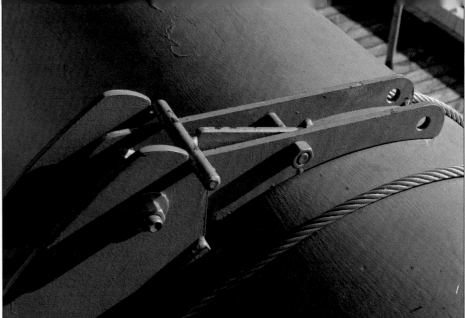

The links for the release mechanisms for both retainers of the roll-off rack are visible beneath the torpedo.

Engine room escape hatches were added to both sides of the amidships deck beginning with the PT-625–660 class. Specifications for this class of boats called for cast aluminum doors, each with three bronze inner handles. This door, forward of the aft starboard torpedo on PT-658, has instead three locking latches controlled by a central handle.

The top of one of the cradles of a torpedo rack and the cables are shown in close-up. The roll-off rack not only dispensed with the old heavy Mark XVIII torpedo tube, but also eliminated the necessity of lubricating the outside of the torpedo or using black powder to eject the torpedo from the tube.

Torpedo Data

	Mark VIII, Mods 3C, 3D	Mark XIII
Design	Bliss-Leavitt	Bliss-Leavitt
Primary Use	DD, DE, PT	Aerial, PT
Power	Turbine	Turbine
Diameter	21 inches	22.5 inches
Length	256.3 inches	161 inches
Weight	3,150 lbs (ready status)	2,216 lbs
Range	13,500 yards (acceptance)	6,300 yards
Speed	36 knots	33.5 knots
Warhead	385 lbs TNT	600 lbs Torpex
Exploder	Mk 3 contact	Mk 8 contact
Builders	Naval Torpedo Station, Newport, RI. Naval Torpedo Station, Alexandria, VA. Naval Gun Factory, Washington, D.C.	Naval Torpedo Station, Newport, RI. Pontiac Motor Division. Ameritorp Corporation. International Harvester.

The fantail of PT-658 is armed with a 40mm Bofors cannon and two depth charges on roll-off racks. At the center of the deck at the stern is a smoke generator. (Jim Alexander)

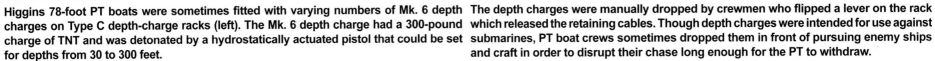

Higgins 78-foot PT boats were sometimes fitted with varying numbers of Mk. 6 depth charges on Type C depth-charge racks (left). The Mk. 6 depth charge had a 300-pound charge of TNT and was detonated by a hydrostatically actuated pistol that could be set for depths from 30 to 300 feet.

The depth charges were manually dropped by crewmen who flipped a lever on the rack which released the retaining cables. Though depth charges were intended for use against submarines, PT boat crews sometimes dropped them in front of pursuing enemy ships and craft in order to disrupt their chase long enough for the PT to withdraw.

At the center of the deck at the stern of PT-658 is a smoke generator. It operated by spewing titanium tetrachloride, which produced a thick "smoke" when it made contact with the water or moisture in the air. Smoke screens were useful in masking the location and bearing of the boat during a daylight attack or escape.

The transoms of the Higgins 78-foot PT boats were clear of the mufflers and exhausts that cluttered the transoms of Elco PT boats. Exhausts on the Higgins PT boats were on the side of the vessel. There is a stern light on a stanchion on the other side of the smoke generator.

In the latter part of World War II, single 40mm Bofors automatic cannons were sometimes fitted on the fantails of Higgins PT boats. By the time the PT-625–660 class was in production, these guns were being installed during production. These guns packed a powerful punch and were particularly useful in barge-busting operations.

The gunner in the port seat of the 40mm cannon controlled the elevation of the piece and fired it using a foot pedal. This is his speed-ring sight.

The 40mm Bofors gun was fed by four-round ammunition clips. With a maximum cyclic rate of fire of 160 rounds per minute, firing was as fast as a loader could insert the clips into the autoloader atop the gun's receiver. At the lower left is the flange of the gun's port trunnion.

This is the lateral pointer's sight. He sat on the starboard side of the 40mm cannon and controlled the traverse of the piece.

Viewing the aft end of the 40mm Bofors mount, the loader's platform with diamond tread is at the bottom, and to the front of it are the gunner's and lateral pointer's seats and the hand-operated elevating and traversing cranks. The frame in the foreground is the depression rail for the 40mm gun.

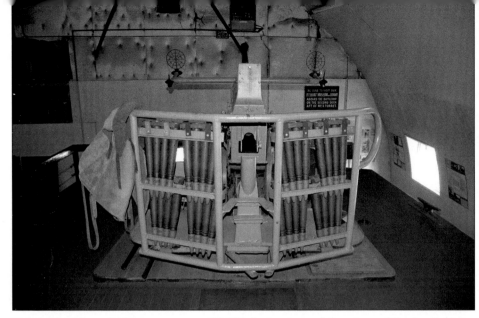

This is the 40mm Bofors cannon on PT-796, facing toward the stern of the boat. At the rear of the loader's platform is a guard rail that does double-duty as a ready rack for four-round clips of 40mm ammunition. The gun's mount is fastened to a wooden foundation built up from the deck.

This replica of an ammunition stowage box is on the port side of the after deck of PT-658, aft of the forward torpedo. To the far right is part of one of the cowl ventilators that supplied air to the engine room. The aft portions of the Mk. 13 torpedoes would have been left in natural metal finish on a World War II PT boat.

The small lever at the center of the inboard side of the aft port depth-charge rack released the cable holding the depth charge in place, sending it to its underwater destination. A system of pulleys within the rack allowed the cable to be drawn tightly, holding the depth charge secure.

A Mk. 13 torpedo on PT-796 displays its bronze afterbody (the section to the rear of the air flask portion of the torpedo), fins, and four-blade counter-rotating propellers. The 2,216-lb. Mk 13, together with its launcher, weighed less than half the total weight its predecessor on PT boats, the Mk 8 torpedo, with its tube.

The circular plate on top of the torpedo casing to the front of the fin holds the starting toggle. A torpedoman would flip the toggle to turn on the engine before the torpedo was launched. Other round plates allowed access to the gyro gears, depth-setter, and other mechanisms. The cable-release lever is on the near side of the torpedo rack.

The weight savings of the lighter Mk 13 torpedo, plus the discontinuation of bulky, heavy torpedo tubes, made possible the mounting of additional weapons on PT boats.

The Mk. 13 torpedo on PT-796 shows an accurate World War II appearance of a natural bronze casing, fins, and propellers and a gray warhead. This model of torpedo was introduced to PT boats around late 1943.

Two performance characteristics of the Mk. 13 torpedo, its range of 6,300 yards and speed of 33½ knots, were inferior to those of the Mk. 8 torpedo, but the Mk. 13 was far more accurate. Its 600-pound warhead was filled with Torpex, a powerful explosive.

In a view facing aft of the two port torpedoes on PT-658, the perforated lug at the very front of the torpedo is the nose piece. Its purpose was to facilitate the handling of the warhead. The late version of the Mk. 13 torpedo weighed 2,216 pounds.

A cowling vent and engine room escape hatch are on the port side of the deck amidships. Specifications called for the oblong door, which has a cast aluminum frame, to measure 16⅝ inches by 19½ inches – just enough room for a crewman to squeeze through.

Operating from Bougainville Island, New Guinea, this 78-foot Higgins, belonging to MTB Squadron 23, is painted in camouflage Measure 31 and is well suited for operations close to shore and for vessels, such as the PTs, that stayed in small ports during the day and ventured out at night. One of this unit's boats (PT-283) was sunk by a coastal battery. PT-279 was involved in a collision with PT-282, but with the exception of PT-278, the remainder were burned on 26 November 1945 to dispose of them.

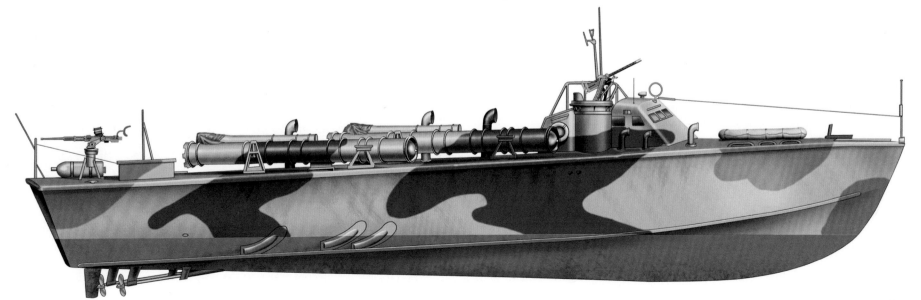

The carburetors of the big Packards gulped plenty of air even at idle, and numerous vents, including this cowl vent amidships on the port side, were situated on the deck over the engine room for that purpose. To the right is the open engine room cover, with the built-in framing for the engine room hatch visible.

The port turret is viewed from aft with the .50-caliber machine guns at maximum elevation. Flash suppressors are fitted over the muzzles. To the left is the engine room cover, with its interior painted white. To the right is the opening over the engine room, with a temporary safety rail set up.

The port .50-caliber machine guns of PT-658 are loaded with belted ammunition. Jutting out from either side of the gun cradle are the upper ammunition guides, which kept the ammunition belts properly routed even as the guns were moved around. The charging handles on the sides of the guns have wooden grips.

A ring-and-bead gun sight is mounted on the Mk. 9 cradle, with both pieces of the sight being visible in profile. Details of the perforated jackets over the barrels and the flash suppressors are in view. Earlier PT boats sometimes had cylindrical flash suppressors on the .50-caliber machine guns.

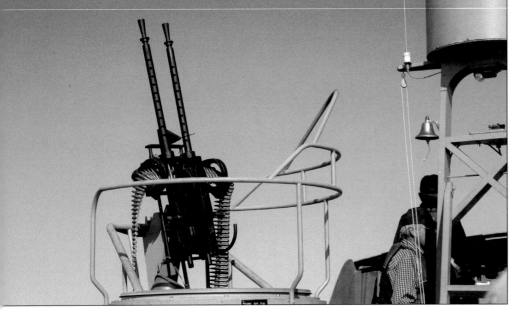

The depression rails on PT boats were intended to physically limit the direction of the gun barrels so gunners would not inadvertently shoot up parts of their own boat. The depression rails on the port machine gun turret were designed to protect the deck, chart house, bridge, and radar mast from overenthusiastic gunners.

In this view up into a .50-caliber machine gun turret on a Higgins PT boat, the bottom of the port ammunition box is to the left, the starboard ammunition box is at center, and the pedestal is between them. The internal wooden framing of the turret is also visible.

For the .50-caliber depression rails on Higgins PT boats, 16-gauge galvanized steel tubing with an outside diameter of 1 inch was specified. Steel plates used on the depression rails were also of galvanized steel. Part of the starboard turret's depression rail is to the right.

On the superstructure aft of the turret is an intake louver for supplying forced-air ventilation below decks. Forward of the louvered vent is the hatch to the port turret. Hand rails are distributed along the superstructure and turret.

Looking to the port side of the bridge of PT-658, lockers are to the left, the helm (or steering wheel) and instruments are at the center, and the door to the chartroom is at the right. The top of the windscreen follows the same contours as the top of the chart house below it.

When photographed, PT-796's bridge layout was similar to that of PT-658, except that it lacked the compasses. To the starboard side of the helm is an electrical switch panel containing the engine ignition switches, fuse box, light switches, and other controls. The locker doors to the port side have piano hinges at their tops.

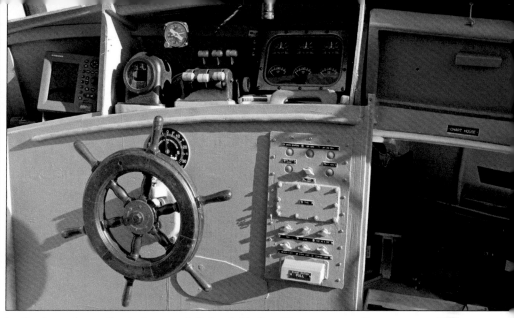

In the bay above the helm are, left to right, the Pioneer magnetic compass, flux-gate gyrocompass repeater, throttle and telegraph bridge control assembly, and an instrument panel containing three tachometers and three manifold pressure gauges. The other instruments are current-day navigational equipment.

On the throttle and telegraph bridge control assembly (center), the three throttle controls are at the top, and at the bottom front are the controls that telegraphed directional orders to the engine room. Pulling these controls up signaled to proceed ahead; the center position signified stop, and the lower position signified to reverse engines.

The radar mast of PT-658 is viewed from the forward starboard side of the chart house, with the top of the windscreen at the bottom of the photo. Although inaccurate for a Higgins boat of the PT-625–660 class, it is similar to a style of mast and radome used on PT boats with SO-type radar units during World War II. The masthead and anchor light is below the radome.

Regardless of the type of radar mast on a PT boat, it was hinged at the bottom and equipped with an after brace, to enable it to be lowered when passing under bridges or other low objects. The late-type radar mast would have had a box-shaped transmitter-receiver unit toward the bottom and an abundance of exposed wiring.

To the starboard side of the bridge of PT-796 is the searchlight and stanchion, with the power cable plugged into a receptacle to the right of the stanchion. On late-production Higgins boats with Mk. 50 5-inch rocket launchers, the Mk. 13 Mod. 2 rocket launcher control panel was installed below the windscreen to the port side of the searchlight.

The radar mast of PT-658 is viewed from down in the engine room with the engine room cover removed. To either side of the photograph are the inboard sides of the .50-caliber machine gun turrets. An improvised guard rail made of rope and bar clamps is set up around the engine room opening.

As seen from below and aft, the PT-658 mast has a modern fire alarm under the radome. A boat's bell is mounted on the mast; these were generally packed away when the boat operated in combat zones, as its ringing could disclose the presence of the boat to the enemy.

The engine room cover is shown installed on PT-796. Removing this cover provided access from above to the engine room, and it was through this single opening that all three engines were removed or reinstalled when necessary. Note the width and fore-and-aft direction of the accurate deck planking.

The engine room cover of PT-658 is shown in place. Like the same cover on PT-796, its edges are bound with metal. Built into the after part of the cover is a square hatch and door for crew access to the engine room, while a deadlight (a small deck light) is on the opposite end.

Four hinged grab handles are screwed to the engine room cover near its corners. The metal binding around the cover is also visible.

Looking down at the forward bulkhead of the engine room with that compartment's cover removed, the engine room instrument panel is at the center. Surrounding it are fuel lines. At either side of the instrument panel are freshwater expansion tanks, part of the fresh-water cooling system; there was one expansion tank for each engine.

With the engine room cover removed, the construction of its interior framing is apparent. To the left of the cover is the framing for the hatch, and the round opening for the deadlight is to the right. A weatherproof gasket is attached around the perimeter of the cover.

The port wing Packard engine is to the lower left of this view into the forward port corner of the engine room. The yellow cylinder toward the bottom is a fuel filter.

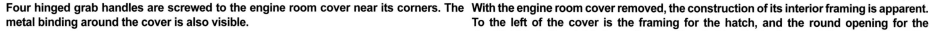

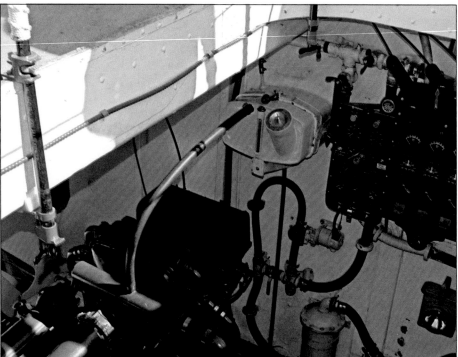

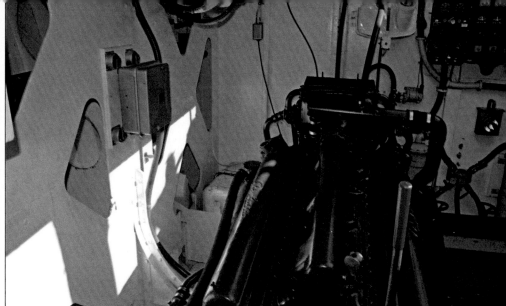

The port wing Packard 4M-2500 engine is viewed from overhead, with the forward end of the engine to the right. The two wing engines are mounted forward of the front of the center engine. The exhaust lines to the left exit through the port side of the hull.

The Packard logo is embossed on the valve covers of the engines, and the exhaust lines are routed from the rear of the starboard wing engine to the exhaust ports on the side of the hull. Directly below the freshwater expansion tank at left are the air filter and carburetor. Mounted on the front of the engine is the supercharger.

The port wing engine is viewed from aft. The engine transmissions were manually shifted to forward, neutral, or astern, in accordance with signals from the bridge. The orange handle in the foreground is part of a replacement shifting lever. The plywood bulkhead to the left is built out from the hull.

This is the starboard wing engine, with the ladder to the engine room hatch at right. The Packard 4M-2500 engines in early PT boats developed 1,200 horsepower, but later engine models installed in later production PT boats reached 1,500 horsepower.

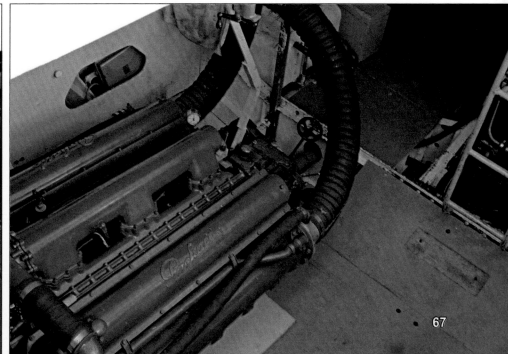

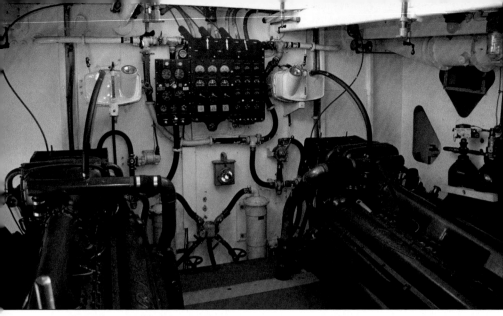

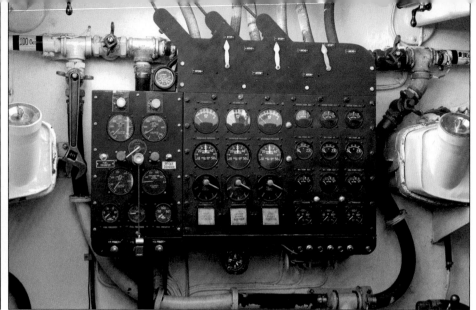

In a view of the forward end of the engine room from aft of the port wing engine, cooling water lines are routed from the freshwater expansion tanks to the engines. The Higgins boats had both a saltwater and a fresh-water engine-cooling system. The red carbon dioxide bottles to the right are part of the fixed fire extinguisher system.

One of several ventilation ducts in the engine room is at the top center of the photo. Below the instrument panel is a hand lantern, to the bottom left of which is the yellow-painted fuel manifold. On the other side of the forward bulkhead are the two forward fuel tanks, between which is the officers' lavatory.

Above the engine room instrument panel are dial indicators, one for each engine and actuated by the telegraph controls on the bridge, which signaled if the engines were to be in shifted into forward, neutral, or reverse gear. The port side of the instrument panel includes fuel gauges and switches; the larger panel on the starboard side includes engine gauges and starter switches.

The air cleaner for the starboard wing engine is at the left. Below it, the carburetor is partially visible. At the center is the top of the supercharger; this unit was a centrifugal, gear-driven model. A simple wooden clamp holds the carbon dioxide tanks in place.

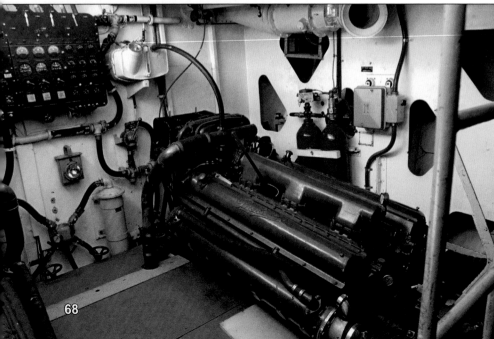

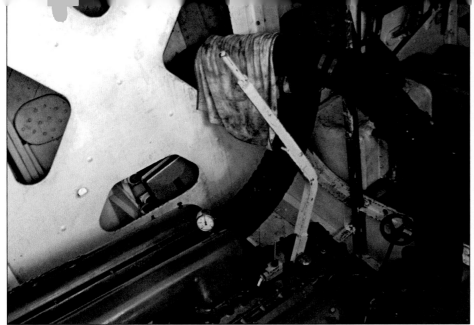

The starboard wing engine's two exhaust lines cross each other aft of the engine and then are routed to the mufflers below the waterline on the side of the hull. At the center is the transmission shift lever.

Viewed between the aft ends of the wing engines, aft of the ladder to the engine room hatch is the center engine. The Higgins 78-foot PT boat has a more spacious engine room than that on the Elco 80-foot boat. Behind the center engine are its exhaust lines.

In a view of the engine room facing forward from the port side of the center engine, the framing of the main deck is visible at the top. To the upper left is the port ventilation duct. The interior of the boat, including the engine room, had a coat of primer topped with two coats of fire-retardant white paint. Decks were coated with nonskid deck paint.

The generator and distribution switchboard is on the starboard side of the engine room adjacent to the center engine. At the top are a voltmeter and ammeters for various electrical systems. Below are switches for electrical systems. The box to the right of the panel is the current-limiting resistor.

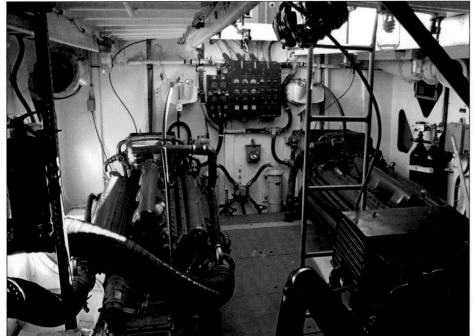

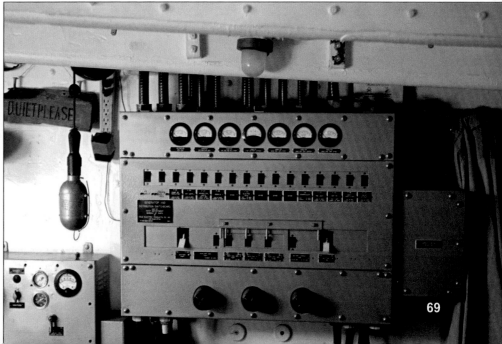

Immediately forward of the generator and distribution switchboard is the control panel for the starboard auxiliary generator. This generator would have been mounted on the deck below the control panel, and for the PT-625–660 class, there would have been an auxiliary generator and control panel on the port side as well.

Life jackets are hanging on the after bulkhead of the engine room. At the center is an intercom speaker, and to the right of it is the fresh-water expansion tank for the center engine; it is of a different design than the two expansion tanks on the forward bulkhead. Small semicircular shelves are on the corners of the bulkhead.

The port ventilation duct is at the center of this view of the forward port corner of the engine room. Triangular cutouts in the longitudinal bulkheads on the sides of the engine room offer access to the spaces between the bulkheads without sacrificing strength.

In the rearmost compartment of the Higgins PT boat, the lazarette, is the steering gear. The steering shaft, controlled from the bridge, enters the steering gearbox (bottom center; the shaft is out of the view), and an arm on top of the gearbox moves the short drag link connected to the port rudder's tiller (right). The large drag link in turn moves the starboard tiller (out of view to the left).

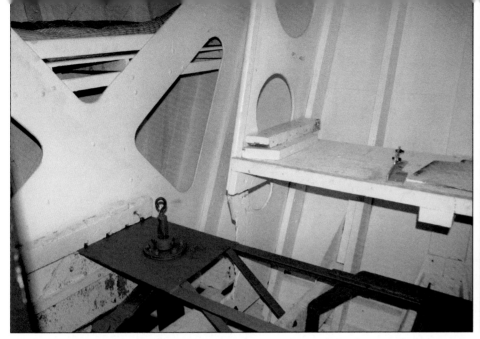

The starboard tiller of PT-658 is the dark gray arm toward the lower left. The rudder shafts and their attached tillers are supported by the gray framework, which runs across the rear of the lazarette. The transom is to the right of the photo, and to the left is a berth.

The door of the hatch to the wardroom is shown closed. To the upper right is the lower part of the turret, with an electrical receptacle mounted on it.

On the deck in the aft starboard part of the bridge is a hatch to the wardroom. The door to the hatch is open in this photo. Its interior is painted white. Two small lockers are built into the starboard bulwark of the bridge.

With the door open, the red-painted ladder leading from the bridge down to the wardroom is visible. As with other deck hatches, a coaming surrounds the hatch, to keep water on the deck from running down into the compartment below.

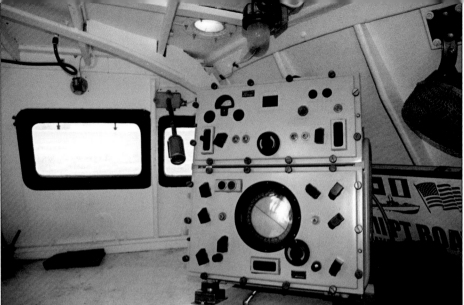

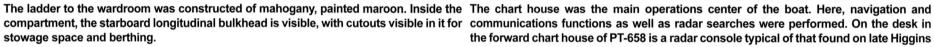

The ladder to the wardroom was constructed of mahogany, painted maroon. Inside the compartment, the starboard longitudinal bulkhead is visible, with cutouts visible in it for stowage space and berthing.

To the starboard side of the radar console on the chart house desk are, left to right, an ammunition display; gyro compass; Collins Type COL-46159 radio receiver, Type 52245 transmitter, and, above the transmitter, a Type 47205 antenna loading coil, all three components being part of the TCS radio set; and, at the lower right, a plotting board. At the bottom is the hatch to the galley and crew's quarters.

The chart house was the main operations center of the boat. Here, navigation and communications functions as well as radar searches were performed. On the desk in the forward chart house of PT-658 is a radar console typical of that found on late Higgins PT boats. The console comprises indicator and accessories-control units.

On the port side of the aft bulkhead of the chart house are, top, a recent-model 12-volt distribution panel added during restoration of the boat, and at the bottom, a fuse panel, with signal-system feed fuses on the left and lights feed fuses on the right. To the right is the aft port side window of the chart house.

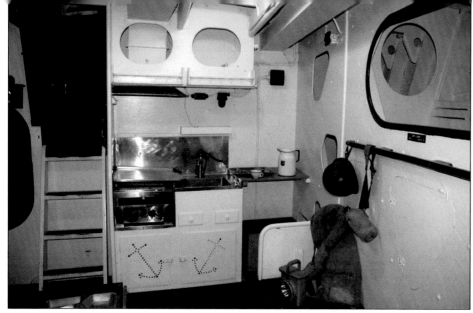

In the galley, facing aft, the ladder to the chart house is to the left of the stove and sink. To the far left is the hatch to the wardroom. The refrigerator/freezer that was installed to the right of the sink on Higgins PT boats in World War II is missing from PT-796.

The galley and the crew's quarters of the Higgins 78-foot PT boats share a common compartment. Berths for four crewmen are nestled between the longitudinal bulkheads and the inner sides of the hull on both sides of the compartment. Below the berth is a hand rail. To the rear of the berth is an electric ventilating fan; in the tropics it could get very hot and dank below decks.

In PT-658's galley, the refrigerator/freezer is installed to the right, and a different arrangement of sink and stove is used, with the sink to the left. The sink provided fresh water using a hand pump. Over and below the sink and oven are storage racks and cupboards. As the boat was originally equipped, a motor generator for the gyro-compass system would have been mounted on a bracket on the bulkhead aft of the ladder.

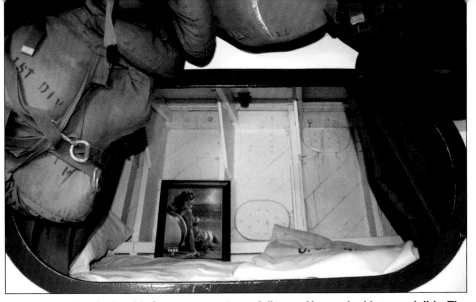

Above the electric fan and the electrical receptacle is a ventilation duct. In addition to the deck-vent and the forced-air ventilation systems, there was a forced-air heating system with its own set of ducts. In particular, the heating system proved to be a real boon to the crews who operated Higgins PT boats in the Aleutians.

A drop-leaf mess table is at the center of the crew compartment, and a correct type of aluminum swing-down ladder is mounted overhead adjacent to the hatch on the main deck (upper right). Toward the bottom is a transom berth; there was one on each side of the compartment, and they served as combination mess seats and berths for four men.

Within a crew berth, the side frames, gussets, and diagonal inner planking are visible. The inner layer of planking was mahogany on most Higgins boats, but some late-production boats used spruce instead. The oval plates on the hull are butt blocks, fastened with bronze screws over butt joints in the planking that occurred between the side frames, to reinforce the joints.

A modification in the PT-625–660 class was the aluminum beams and gussets installed below the wooden beams of the main deck in the crew compartment to reinforce the foredeck below the 37mm cannon. Between the recessed berths and lockers on both sides of the crew compartment, vertical aluminum stanchions supported the beams.

Because of the tapering of the crew compartment toward the forward end, the transom berths almost meet in this area. These combination seats and berths originally were fitted with cushions covered with Pantasote, an imitation leather. To the right is the bulkhead between the forepeak and crew compartment.

At the aft starboard corner of the crew compartment, a berth is inset behind the longitudinal bulkhead, while the aft bulkhead of the compartment, fitted with several shelves, is to the right. An M1 helmet is hanging from the hand rail.

The crew's transom berths (the starboard forward one is shown) have mahogany plywood tops with small removable panels with finger holes, allowing the insides of the structures to be used for stowage. To the right is the starboard vertical stanchion for the reinforcing beams for the 37mm gun on the foredeck.

An oval door is provided for the hatch through the watertight bulkhead between the crew's quarters. The door has cross-bracing and two locking handles. A coat locker is to the right. Through the hatch, the drop-leaf table in the crew quarters is visible.

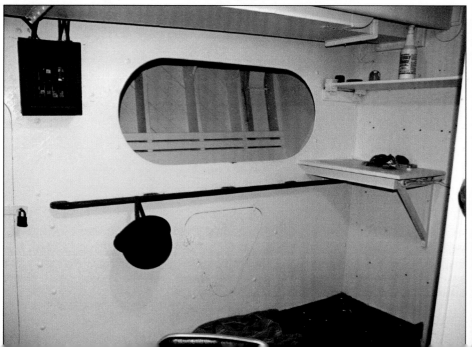

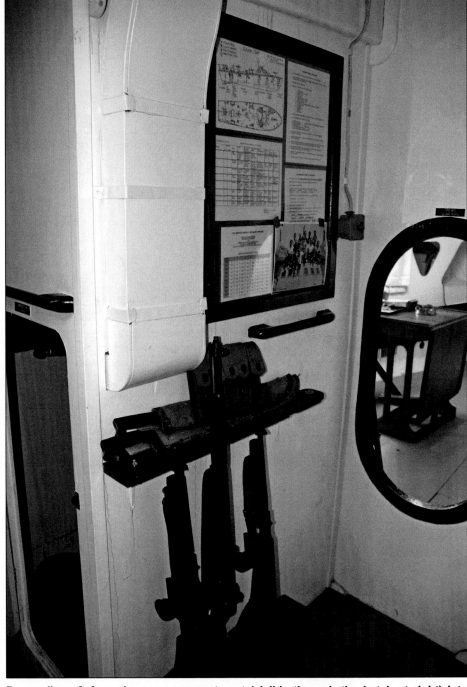

The crew's head is in the aft starboard section of the crew quarters. Here part of the toilet is visible. The sink is located in the cubbyhole within the triangular cutout in the longitudinal bulkhead. A vertical hand rail and mirror are attached to the longitudinal bulkhead.

Proceeding aft from the crew compartment (visible through the hatch at right) into the wardroom, one first passes the ammunition locker, the opening to which is at the lower left. On the side of the locker is a weapons rack with two Thompson .45-caliber submachine guns, a Garand M1 rifle, and machetes.

Looking aft through the hatch in the aft bulkhead of the crew compartment, the wardroom is visible. The ladder leads up to the bridge. The electronics mounted to the left of this ladder on PT-625–660 class boats were components of the IFF (identification, friend or foe) system, which was a means of positively identifying friendly aircraft or naval craft.

In the berth on the starboard side of the wardroom, a manhole is cut through the bulkhead to give access to the forward fuel tanks compartment. The round, gas-tight plywood cover of the manhole has been removed. A similar manhole was specified for the opposite side of the wardroom.

Behind the starboard longitudinal bulkhead in the wardroom (left) is an officer's berth, with a mahogany step fastened to the bulkhead for ease of access. Below the berth is stowage space—an arrangement similar to the berths and lockers in the crew's quarters. To the right is the weapons rack.

The door to the ammunition locker in the wardroom is open, revealing shelves full of wooden and metal ammunition boxes as well as some decidedly non-regulation luxuries. At the bottom is a box for 350 rounds of .50-caliber ammunition. Directly above the ammunition locker structure is the well of the chart house.

This is the forward port corner of the wardroom, with the ammunition locker to the right. A transom berth (lower right) runs along this side of this compartment. Stowed on the deck are several 40mm ammunition containers, with empty 40mm casings in clips on top.

The ceiling of the wardroom also comprises the main deck framing and decking, which is oriented diagonally. The inner layer of decking, seen here, is ⅜-inch by 5½-inch mahogany. To the lower left is the bookcase on the port side of the aft bulkhead of the wardroom.

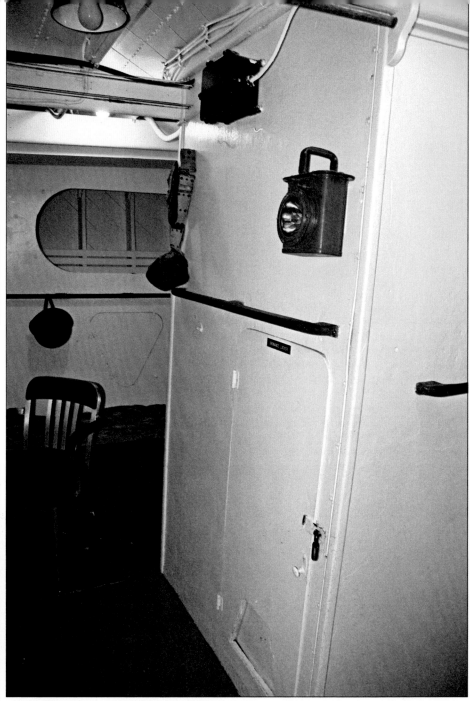

The ammunition locker in the wardroom is shown with the door closed and padlocked. In actual practice, a folding mess table was stored on the locker to the left of the locker door and below the hand rail. Above the hand rail is a hand lantern.

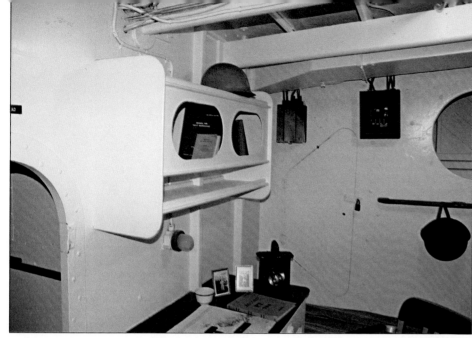

The bookcase on the aft bulkhead of the wardroom is mounted over a built-in desk with drawers on PT-796. The vertical pieces running up through the bookcase and to the right of it are bulkhead stiffeners. At the center is a locker door in the longitudinal bulkhead.

The door to the officer's head is hinged on the inside of that compartment and opens into it. To the lower left is a portable fire extinguisher. The lavatories and sinks on the PT boat were supplied from freshwater tanks, and the toilets used sea water.

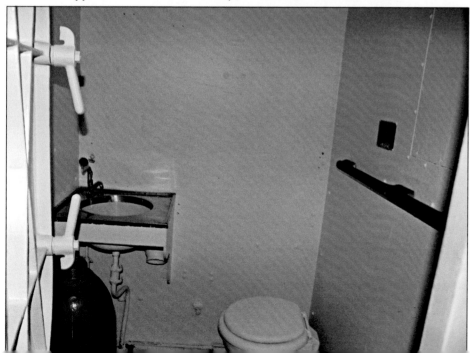

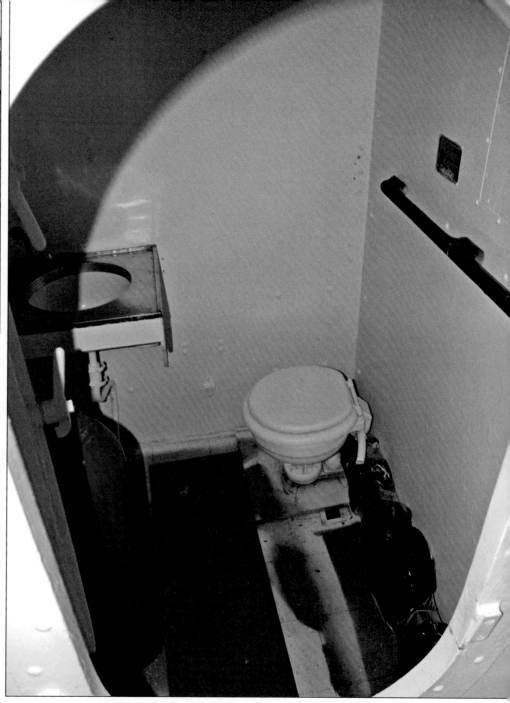

The officers' head was a spartan affair with a lavatory and toilet, each operated by a hand pump. A mahogany hand rail is on the wall. This head was nestled in between the forward fuel tanks, located aft of the wardroom.

Today there are fewer than a half-dozen surviving Higgins 78-foot torpedo boats. Three are in museums, permanently in the dry. PT-658, restored by Save the PT Boat, Inc., in Portland, Oregon, is the only restored Higgins PT in operating condition. (Jim Alexander)